A Chris Adventure Book

CHRIS'S FAMILY VACATION AT ROCKET WORLD

STORY BY: J. LEW
ILLUSTRATED BY: MISHA

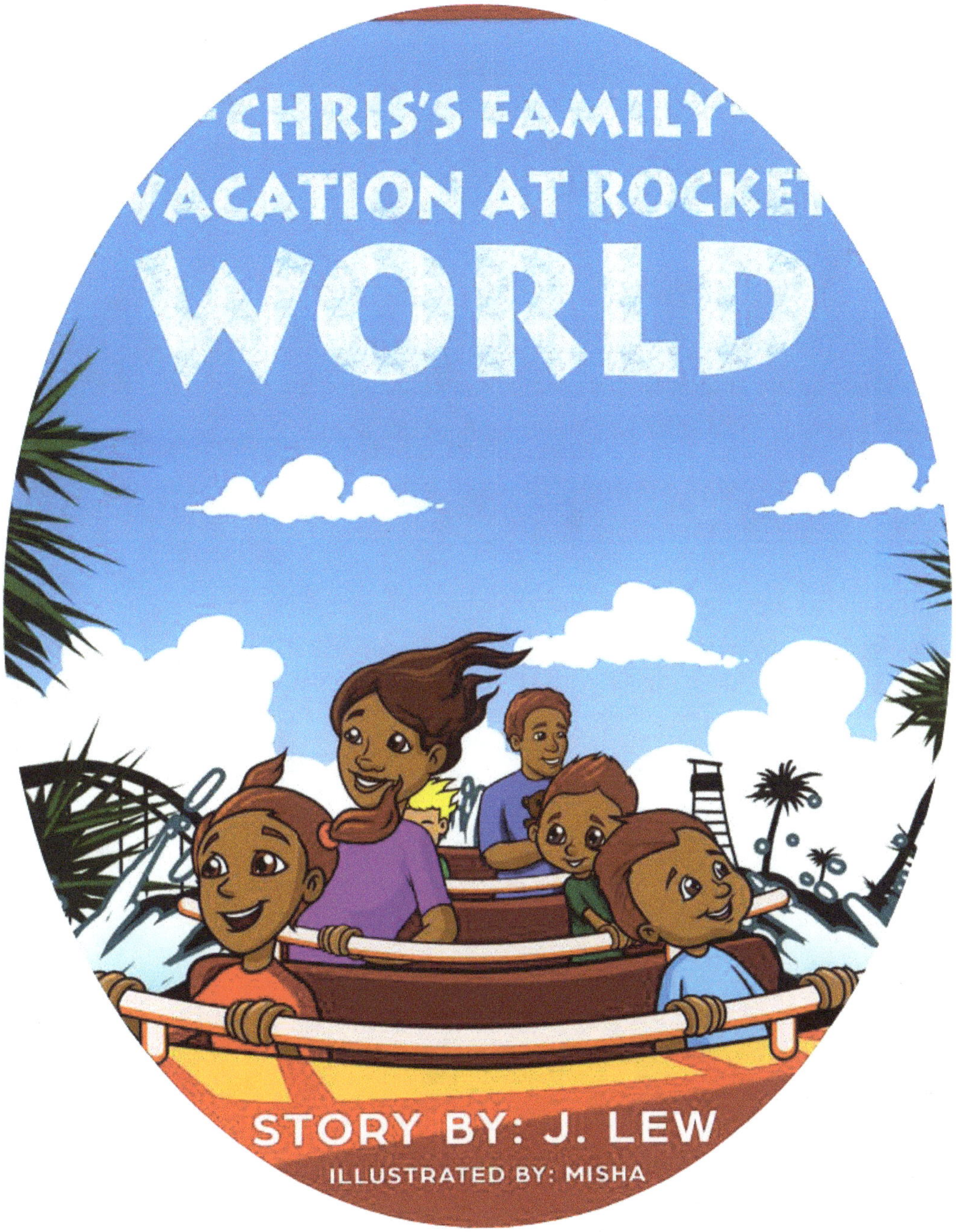

Copyright © 2022 by J. Lew

Chris's Family Vacation At Rocket World
By J. Lew

Printed in United States of America

ISBN 9781946806109

All rights are reserved solely by the author. No part of this book may be reproduced, or transmitted in any form or by any means without the written permission from the author.

www.jlew-books.com

Today, Chris and his family are traveling to Florida. Chris is so excited about going to Rocket World that he trips over their luggage.

"Ugh," Chris groans when he falls.

Toni and Danny think he's funny and laughs.

"Alright, Chris," Mom says.

"I'm okay." He says and jumps up. "I'm ready to go." He says excitedly.

They pack their luggage into the van and drive to the Airport.

Chris and Danny watch the airplanes as they take off and land from their terminal window.
"Look how big they are," Chris points out.
"Yes, and they are bigger than our house." Says Danny.

Chris sits at the window on the plane.
"Wow, I can see the whole world from here!" He shouts.
"Chris." His mother calls. "Not so loud." She whispers.
"I'm sorry, mom," Chris apologizes.

Chris and his family arrive at the Florida airport. Now they are standing at the carousel waiting on their luggage.

"It'll be cool to ride on the luggage." Says Danny.

"Let's try it." Says Chris.

"Oh, no, you don't," Mom stops both of them.

"Ahhh," Danny and Chris sigh.

"Stand back, both of you," Mom demands.

Chris is upset and pouts.

Toni takes Chris aside, pointing at the airplanes taking off. Danny helps load the luggage into the van.
"Toni, I love to fly, do you?" Chris asks.
"Yes, it was fun." She says.
"I'm going to be a pilot someday," Chris tells her.

Finally, they arrive at the hotel. They cannot wait to get to their room. After checking in, they take the elevator to the second floor and walk to their room.

Toni is the first to the door. "I'll open the door."

"That's not fair," Danny and Chris complain.

"I can't help if I walk faster than you," Toni opens the door.

Toni takes charge. "Danny and Chris, you will sleep on the sleeper couch, and I'll sleep on the sleeper chair."
"Okay." Agrees Danny and Chris. "Our bed is bigger than your bed." Says Danny.
"Now that we know where we are sleeping, it's time to go shopping." Says Toni ignoring Danny.
"Right now, we are going to get a little rest. We'll go shopping later." Says mom.
"Okay." Says Toni. "We'll watch TV until it's time to leave."

After everyone has rested, they go into town to see the sights.
"We should look both ways before crossing the street." Says Chris.
"We must wait for the red light before we step into the crosswalk." Says Toni.
"That's Right," Dad Says. "Safety is first."

Chris and Danny are very tired and fall fast asleep, dreaming of Rocket World.
Toni stays awake for a while, listening to music on her tablet.

Chris and his family have arrived at Rocket world at last. They take a picture in front of the Rocket World fountain.

"Come on, everybody, let's go," Chris shouts.

"We will, but let's take our picture first." Says mom.

On the first day, they visit the little Astronauts Park.
"I'm going to ride everything!" Shouts Danny.
"I'm going to ride everything, too," Chris replies.

From the Farris Wheel, they can see many rides in the park.

"Mom, I can see all of Rocket World from here." Says Chris excitedly.

"This is fun." Says Danny.

"I can't wait to get on the roller coasters." Says Toni.

"Giddy up, Snowy." Says Chris.
"No, I was going to name mine Snowy." Cries Danny.
Toni Says. "I'm naming mine Maximus."
Snowy and Maximus are horses on their grandparent's ranch.

The Alien ride goes through the moon. Danny and Chris are having lots of fun.
"This is fun." Shouts Danny.
"I'm having the most fun ever!" Chris Shouts.

After all the walking and standing in line, everyone is ready to eat lunch.
"Okay, everyone, I want you to eat your food," Mom tells them.
"Can we get on more rides?" Asks Chris.
"Yes, Chris, we'll get on more rides, so eat your food." Says Dad.

Everyone enjoys the airplane ride, but Chris doesn't feel as safe on this airplane.
"Weeeee!" shouts Danny excitedly.
"We're going too high," Chris shouts worriedly.
"Just hold on, Chris!" Shouts Toni.

"Danny is driving too slow; I don't think he can reach the peddle," Toni tells her dad.
"I'm the best driver in the world," Danny says as he swerves in the lane.
"Faster, Danny, faster. Dad and Toni are catching us." Says Chris.

On the second day, Toni is finally on the roller coaster and having a blast. "Now, this is what I'm talking about." Shouts Toni. "We're getting back in line when we finish, right, dad?"

"We'll see what my stomach says first," Dad says as the roller coaster shakes and bumps in every turn.

The water ride gets everyone wet as it roars through the waterfall.
"Whoa, I don't think Toby likes to get wet," Chris Shouts.
"We'll dry him off when we get back to the hotel." Says mom.
"Toby would like that a lot," Chris replied.

"I don't see any sea monsters." Says Chris.
"I'm sure we'll see some soon," Danny assures him.
"There's no such thing as sea monsters," Toni says.
"Look at all the beautiful fish, guys," Mom changes the subject.
"I like all of them," Chris points to many of the coral reef fish.

"Wow." Says Toni, Danny, and Chris as they walk through the aquarium.
"We must be in the biggest aquarium in the whole wide world." Says Danny.
"It is very big, but it is not the largest," Dad explains.
"We need to put one of these in our backyard," Chris says.
"I don't think so," Mom says quickly. "We'll just have to visit the one closer to home."
"That will be fun, and we can go to the zoo," Chris says.
"We'll think about it," Mom says.

Chris and Toby are the first to splash down.
"Whoa." Says Chris.
"I'm coming, Chris." Says dad as he jumps from his float to help Chris.
"We'll just float slowly down the river," Mom says to assure him.

On their third day, they visit the Astronauts Hall.
"I'm going to go into outer space someday with Toby," Chris says.
"That will be great, Chris. You'll get to see what the earth looks like from space," Dad encourages him.
"Don't forget all the stars and space aliens," Chris says.
Toni rolls her eyes and laughs.

The tram ride takes them through the dimensions of outer space. They will see the planets, moons, and stars.
"The swirls are so pretty," Toni says.
"I can't wait to see the space aliens," Chris says.
"Me too." Says Danny.
"I know all the planets and moons by heart," Chris says.

Chris and his family take in a stage play about two aliens from different worlds who find a way to be friends forever.
Their dad is tired and falls asleep during the show. Everyone else loves the show, and when it's over, they shout and applaud, waking their dad from his nap.

The train ride takes them back to the front of the park.
"I'm going to be a train driver one day," Chris informs everyone.
"They are called Railroad Engineers," Dad corrects Chris.
"Yes, I'm going to be one someday," Chris assures them.
"You can be whatever you want," Mom encourages Chris.

It's fireworks night at Rocket World, and Toni, Danny, and Chris are excited. "Whoa," Chris shouts. "That one was the biggest."
"They are all big," Toni and Danny Shouts. "They are so pretty," Toni shouts.

"We have a few more days to go here at Rocket World." Says Chris. "I hope to see you on my next adventure. Bye for now, see you soon."

A Chris Adventure Book

More books by J. Lew
I'm Not Afraid Of The Dark
Sunken Treasures
Little Ranch Hands

J. Lew

www.ingramcontent.com/pod-product-compliance
Lightning Source LLC
Chambersburg PA
CBHW051402110526
44592CB00023B/2929